COME CLOSER
AND LISTEN

COME CLOSER AND LISTEN

NEW POEMS

CHARLES SIMIC

ecco

An Imprint of HarperCollins*Publishers*

HarperCollins books may be purchased for educational, business, or sales promotional use. For information, please e-mail the Special Markets Department at SPsales@harpercollins.com.

FIRST EDITION

Designed by Suet Yee Chong

Library of Congress Cataloging-in-Publication Data has been applied for.

ISBN 978-0-06-290846-9

19 20 21 22 23   LSC   10 9 8 7 6 5 4 3 2 1

For Helen

As if one needed eyes in order to see

—RALPH WALDO EMERSON

Contents

III

Some Birds Chirp

Others have nothing to say.
You see them pace back and forth,
Nodding their heads as they do.

It must be something huge
That's driving them nuts--
Life in general, being a bird.

Too much for one little brain
To figure out on its own.
Still, no harm trying, I guess,

Even with all the racket
Made by its neighbors,
Darting and bickering nonstop.

Hide-and-Seek

Haven't found anyone
From the old gang.
They must be still in hiding,
Holding their breaths
And trying not to laugh.

Our street is down on its luck,
Its windows broken here and there
Where on summer nights
We heard couples arguing,
Or saw them dancing to the radio.

The redhead we were
All madly in love with,
Who sat on her fire escape
Smoking late into the night,
Must be in hiding too.

The skinny boy
On crutches
Who always carried a book,
May not have
Gotten very far.

Darkness comes early
This time of year
Making it hard
To recognize familiar faces
Among those of strangers.

Blind Fate

Grabbing someone in the street,
Letting another go scot-free,
Like that crazy old woman
With something urgent to say
You couldn't make any sense of,
Who hooked you by the arm,
Till you tore yourself away,
Only to bump into a beggar
Scattering coins from his cup
And having to listen to him
Chew you out and curse you
In front of all these people.
What comes next, you'll never know.
Blind fate here runs the show.

Come Closer and Listen

I was born--don't know the hour--
Slapped on the ass
And handed over crying
To someone many years dead
In a country no longer on a map,

Where like a leaf in a tree,
The fair weather gone,
I twirled around and fell to the ground
With barely a sound
For the wind to carry me away

Blessed or cursed--who is to say?
I no longer fret about it,
Since I've heard people talk
Of a blind lady called Justice
Eager to hear everyone's troubles,
But don't know where to find her

And ask her the reason
The world treats me some days well,
Some days ill. Still, I'd never
Be the first to blame her.
Blind as she is, poor thing,
She does the best she can.

The Old Orphan

For Andrew Periale

The sparrows in the gutter knew you
And hopped out of the way,
The trash being blown about
By the wind gusting did as well.

A few scenes from your life
Were about to be performed
By a puppet theater in the park,
When it started to rain hard,

Making the great trees panic
Along with mothers and children,
Who ran shrieking for cover
Wherever they could find one,

Except for you, already seated
In a long row of empty chairs,
Waiting for your angry stepfather
To step out from behind a curtain.

Skywalking

Much grief awaits us, friends.
From this day on
We'll be testing our luck
Like a man stretching a wire
Between two skyscrapers,
Who sets out to walk on it
Carrying an open umbrella
Which the wind may snatch away
When he is halfway,
And then have its fun
Bouncing it off walls and windows.
We are likely to forget the man
Waving his arms up there
Like a scarecrow in a squall.

The Fall

One flaps his arms to arrest the fall
One climbs a ladder he brought along
One peeks inside a tattered Bible
One goes on laughing at some joke

One opens a large red umbrella
One grasps at a straw floating in the air
Overjoyed to hold it for a moment
Distraught to see it slip away like that

You up there did you ever save anyone?
A young woman shouts angrily
As she falls alongside her children
Quiet and alone with their thoughts

Summer Night

A swarm of half-naked, tattoo-covered bodies
To squeeze through on the sidewalk,
Past a raised dagger dripping with blood
And a winged serpent paused to attack.

Young boys smoke reefers and shoot baskets
In the dark playground. Drunk old men
Mutter to themselves on park benches
While garish birds and bats flit past them,

Each of whom carries an occult meaning
Their owner would be happy to relate.
Don't be so foolish as to stop and inquire
About the Spider-Man on a shaved head,

Or the angel of death on a girl's back
As they crowd the entrance of a club
Where some dude in a white tux
Has the huge dance floor all to himself.

Metaphysics Anonymous

A storefront mission in a slum
Where we come together at night
To confess our fatal addiction
For knowledge beyond appearances,

Estranged from family and friends
While racking our brains whether
The world we see is truly out there,
Or it never leaves our minds.

The unreality of us asking for help
An additional quandary to ponder
As we line up with bowed heads
For coffee and cookies to be served.

Mad People

Only birds and animals these days
Are sane and worth talking to.
I don't mind waiting for a horse
To stop grazing and hear me out.

Even a tree is better company.
Some oak proud of its branches
Heavy with leaves too polite
To address a stranger above a whisper.

A crow would make a good friend.
The one I have my eye on
Knows me well, but is currently
Busy with something he's spotted

In my neighbor's yard, going over
The scorched ground where
Years ago a dozen hens used to roam
And a rooster who crowed all day.

Soap Bubbles

They tore down the seedy block
Of small, dimly lit shops
With their dusty displays
Of love bracelets, nose rings,
Tarot cards and sticks of incense,
Where once I saw a young man
With blood all over his white shirt
Blow soap bubbles in the air,
His face unruffled and handsome
Save when he puffed his cheeks.

Open Late

A small-town laundromat brightly lit
On a street of darkened storefronts
With an aged Elvis in it studying a page
Of some well-worn girlie magazine.
A few motley clouds in the night sky,
One hovering over like a death mask,
Its hollow eye pits taking it all in,
While his torn jeans spin in the machine.

Psst

Don't go psst
With a finger
Over your lips,
You seated behind me at the movies,
Or in church
Where I bow my head to pray,
Or in this dive
Where I'm the sole customer,
Shushing me
Out of a dark corner
As I hum to myself
With eyes closed
Thinking of God-knows-what.

Astronomy Lesson

The silent laughter
Of the stars
In the night sky
Tells us all
We need to know

Something Evil Is Out There

That's what the leaves are telling us tonight.
Hear them panic and then fall silent,
And though we strain our ears we hear nothing--
Which is even more terrifying than something.

Minutes seem to pass or whole lifetimes,
While we wait for it to show itself
This very moment, or surely the next?
As the trees rush to make us believe

Their branches knocking on the house
To be let in and then hesitating.
All those leaves falling quiet in unison
As if not wishing to add to our fear,

With something evil lurking out there
And drawing closer and closer to us.
The house dark and quiet as a mouse
If one had the nerve to stick around.

Terror

Saw a toad
jump out of boiling water
Saw a chicken
dance on a hot plate
in a penny arcade
Saw Etruscans in a museum
flogging slaves
to the accompaniment
of pipes and flutes
Saw a palm tree
trying to outrun a hurricane
Saw sea waves
rush ashore
some angry
some afraid
of what they'll find
Saw men and women
lose their heads
and search for them everywhere
Saw a feast laid out
on a long table
to which only crows came
Saw a dog go forth
barking like a prophet of old

Saw rats and mice
running terrified
through mazes
heralding
the evils to come

After the Bombing

A great city lay reduced to ruins
As you stirred in a hammock
Closing your eyes and letting
The paper you were reading
Fall out of your hand to the ground,
Where the afternoon breeze
Took an interest in it and swept it
Back and forth across the lawn
Toward the neighboring woods,
So the owls can study the headlines
As soon as night comes
And shriek from time to time,
Making mice shake in their beds.

Arson

Shirts rose on a neighbor's laundry line,
One or two attempting to fly,
As three fire engines sped by
To save a church going up in flames.

People walking back from the pyre
With their Sunday clothes in tatters
Looked like a troupe of scarecrows
The bank had ousted from their farm.

As for the firebug, we were of two minds:
Some kid trying out a new drug,
Or a drunk ex-soldier angry at God
And country for making him a cripple.

Greek Story

For Hugh and Alisa

Where can I cook for these people
Whose boat had sunk at sea
The old woman went around asking
Where can I cook for these people

Huddled together and weeping
Or sitting alone with their grief
Where can I cook for these people
Who sailed to us this stormy day

Heaven doesn't hear the cries
Of the ones drowning but I do
Where can I cook for these people
The old woman went around asking

And the dead washed ashore
Opened their eyes like children
Shaken out of a bad dream
And pressed forward to kiss her hand

Strolling Players

Carrying a coffin of a soldier one dark night
Through a small, sleeping village,
Then filing quietly into someone's yard,
Hoping dogs won't bark, children won't cry
And whoever awakes will look out
As they get set and distribute their parts

To enact without a word being spoken,
A scene from their neighbor's life,
Already remote and unintelligible,
As if he had been a wisp of smoke
That lingered briefly over a rooftop
As our eyes were turned elsewhere

In this land grown numb from its wars,
Forgoing lament and public display of grief,
Save for this dim figure stepping forth
With arms extended as she asks God
For some stage magic to make her boy rise
From where he lies and stroll home with them.

You'll Be Pleased with Our Product

A cage big enough to kennel a man
You wish to remind he's no better
Than a stray dog waiting his turn
To be put to death by the ASPCA.

So that you may rest easy, our cages
Are built with your safety in mind
And are strong enough to withstand
Outbreaks of rage and suicidal despair.

Light Sleeper

You were a witness
To so many crimes
In your lifetime, my friend,
No wonder most nights
You can be found
Testifying at a trial
In some country
Whose language
You don't even speak.

The proceedings
Brutally slow
With more and more corpses
Being brought in
Their ghastly wounds
As you saw them
With your own eyes
And in photographs.

You'll be asked
To return tomorrow,
So once more
You'll stagger out of bed
And grope your way

Toward the silent
Crowded courtroom
Already in session
Just down the hall.

Monsters

After Ovid

For once, the father of the gods,
Thoroughly pissed
By the cheating and lying Cercopes
And their murderous ways,
Wanted to change them
Into screeching monkeys,
But hesitated, grew uncertain,
Considered jackals instead,
Venomous snakes, thinking perhaps
A greasy rat in the sewer
Would fit the type better, in fact:
Going from A to Z in the Bestiary
He couldn't find a single species
To match the vast capacity for evil
Of these awful creatures,
Not even among deadly spiders
And graveyard worms
Who are blameless for their conduct.

In My Church

You are the Lord of the broken,
The ones crucified and bled
During their long night of torture
In a cellar of some prison.

You inspect the instruments
Of cruelty and touch them
In awe at the pride these men
Take in their line of work,

While their wives and mothers
Rise to attend the early Mass,
Where you too must now hurry
Before they find your broken limbs

And face missing from the cross,
One or two candles still burning
In your terrifying absence
Under the dark and majestic dome.

Among My Late Visitors

There is also a cow
Whose eyes the soldiers
Took out with a knife
And lit straw under its tail
So it would run blind
Over a minefield
And thereafter into my head
From time to time

O Great Starry Sky

Where our thoughts go
Like door-to-door Bible salesmen,
Only to have the doors
Slammed into their faces.

At Giubbe Rosse in Florence

For Charles and Holly Wright

He's a wise man who forgoes the future
And savors the here and now
Bent over a bowl of gnocchi
In this joint where at lunchtime
We all order the same steaming dish
Of which every creamy spoonful
Deserves to be licked thoroughly.

Newspapers fallen on the floor
With their screaming headlines
Trampled over by muddy shoes.
The last long sip of wine making
Someone thoughtful, someone else
Smile to themselves as they rise
Searching their pockets for a tip.

Tugboat

Bringing the summer night in
Over the calm and purple sea
As if it were a barge filled with coal.
The rows of widow's walks
Along the rocky coast
Stand white and deserted.
The long-suffering wives
Of whaling ship captains
Lie buried in family graveyards
Dotting the darkening hills.
The bloodshot eye of the setting sun
Keeping watch for them.

The Last Lesson

It will be about nothing.
Not about love or God,
But about nothing.
You'll be like a new kid in school
Afraid to look at the teacher
While struggling to understand
What they are saying
About this here nothing

Meditation in the Gutter

Of things beautiful.
Things fleeting.
Like the scent of summer night
At the corner of Christopher and Bleecker
Silent and deserted

As I stood leaning
Against a mailbox
Where years ago
I dropped a love letter
And never heard back.

When a cat walked up to me,
One of its paws raised
As if to call my attention
To the cunning threads
By which our lives are rigged.

Strange Sweetness

Happy are those who pass their waking hours
Basking in that strange sweetness
That takes away every care in the world,
Except the one that concerns their love

For some man or woman who does not suspect
They are being loved by a stranger,
While they themselves go on brooding
Regarding another clueless person,

The length of an endless summer
Of sweltering days and muggy nights,
When beyond dark open windows,
Many are sleeping naked, alone or in pairs.

My Little Heaven

Why the wrought-iron fence
With nasty-looking spikes
And four padlocks and a chain
Securing the heavy gate?

I stop by from time to time,
To check if it's unlocked
And peek through the bars
At rows of pretty flowers

And its tree-lined promenade
Streaked with sunlight.
One little birdie hopping on it,
Tickled pink about something.

Imponderabilia

I tie myself into knots
Over you, baby.
Sailor's tricky knots
Throughout the night,
Hangman's big one
In dawn's early light.
Plonk, said the leaky gutter
To the fat bucket
Pining down below.

Bed Music

Our love was new
But our bedsprings were old.
On the floor below
They stopped eating
With forks in the air,

While we went on
Playing our favorites:
"Shake It Baby,"
"Slow Boogie,"
"Shout, Sister, Shout."

That was the limit!
They called the cops.
Did you bring beer?
We asked the men in blue
As they broke down the door.

The Henhouse Is on Fire

Castles in the air were his thing.
Seen in Morocco wearing a fez--
Or was it on the North Pole?
Giving a girl a ride in a dogsled.

All hell broke loose back home
After his wife found out,
"The henhouse is on fire"
He told his drinking buddies,

Popping up here and there,
Consulting a fortune-teller in Naples,
Waving from a train in Brazil
And vanishing like the devil himself

An early explorer claimed to have seen
Playing the flute and dancing
On some rock out in the Pacific
No ship afterwards could find again.

The Many Lauras

Alas, I burn and am not believed.
—PETRARCH

I loved three different Lauras,
At one time or another,
They laughed at everything I said,
While I shed tears in secret.

Even in church praying they'd smile
At the memory of me,
Even in the arms of another man
They'd hide their grins,

Or so I imagined, because I never
Laid my eyes on them again.
It was a huge city where one got lost
Easily as they must've done too.

Petrarch, you only loved one Laura
And wrote hundreds of poems to her.
I loved three, but only wrote one
And it's not even a good one.

The American Dream

When Arlene powders her nose
In a mirror on her dresser
And spying her naked breasts
Slips the powder puff lower
To touch one of her nipples,
While some preacher on TV
Asks his congregation to pray
And to send him money today,
This is called The American Dream.

Among the Ruins

You press your nose, old man,
Against a vacant storefront
Like a fish to a porthole of a ship
Rusting on the sea bottom,
Expecting a ghost or two to follow

After you in the deserted street,
As you slip into a movie theater,
Take a seat among its ruins,
Like a much-decorated soldier
In a mausoleum for the war dead,

Before heading for the train station,
Its tower rising like a biblical curse
Amid walls covered with graffiti,
To meet your dapper young father
Coming home on the evening train.

The Judgment

An early ray of light too bright
For any human eye to bear,
As if the night was cut by a knife
About to strike from a rooftop
At the sprawling city below,

Split up couples in doorways,
And force others in their beds
To cover their nakedness,
Before accosting some fellow
Darting out of a small hotel,

Making him stop dead in his tracks
As if he just heard a judge
Pronounce his sentence,
Startling the mannequins in store windows
Along the avenue, wide awake.

Birds of a Feather

I like the black keys better

I like the lights turned down low

I like women who drink alone

While I hunch over the piano

Looking for all the pretty notes

Truck Stop

Death, the pale thief
Who works alone,
Sipping coffee in the rear booth
Of an all-night diner,
While hatching plans
How to rob one of these truckers
Of his life tonight
As he closes his eyes
Over the steering wheel,
Remembering a pretty hitchhiker
Wave goodbye to him
And grow smaller and smaller
In his rearview mirror
Along with fleeing lights.

That Young Fellow

Who befriended a small pebble
He found in his sneaker
One hot summer night,
And held on to it tightly
As he walked the crowded streets
Dragging his sore foot
Past lightly clad men and women
Partying on the sidewalk,
Save for him, slow and in pain
And keen to remain invisible
Till Jesus comes to judge us all,
Unless some giddy miss
Elects to give him a kiss now.

Hey, Loudmouth

Like a suicide
Dangling by one hand
From a parapet,
This spider talks to himself,
Cusses too,
As he sways to and fro
By a thread,
His voice growing louder
In my head
Lying wide awake
In this big old bed.

It's a Day like Any Other

The old couple are weeding
Side by side in the garden,
Their dog right behind them
Wagging his tail eager to help.

Living in complete ignorance
Of what goes on in the world
Is the well-guarded secret
Of their lifelong happiness.

Sleepwalkers in love, watch them
Reach for each other's hand
When their work is done,
Pure as angels and proud as devils.

The Hand That Rocks the Cradle

Time--that murderer
No one has caught yet

Sunday Service

The rooster wears a bishop's miter
While four hens trail after him
Clucking and nodding their heads
In approval of his morning's sermon.

The black and white mutt in the yard
Has found religion too
Barking at a strange cat up in a tree
As if it were the devil himself.

Descartes, I hear, did his best philosophizing
By lazing in bed past noon.
Not me! I'm on my way to the dump,
Waving to neighbors going to church.

Charmed Circle

This banquet
Of golden cake crumbs
Strewn over our breakfast table
Could feed
A flock of wild birds

We ought to
Shake the tablecloth
Out in the yard
And go back to bed
Leaving them
To chirp about their good luck

Not even minding
To take flight
Every time your mother
Sticks a mop
Out of the kitchen door
And gives
Its tousled head a shake

Haystack

Can you find in there
The straw that broke
Your mother's back?

Birds at Dusk

For Adam Zagajewski

The sunset over the lake
Made one of them squawk
And cause others to join
In comparable distress.

"Even birds detest poetry,"
I remember someone saying
Just as they fell quiet
While shadows lengthened on the water
Smothering the fires.

But though we waited
With bated breath
They voiced no further complaints
From their nests.

Sit Tight

When the old clock
That woke the dead
With its loud tick finally fell silent,
Eternity moved in.
A mirror looked toward the door
With eyes of a dog
Pleading to be taken
Out for a long walk.

Late Night Quiz

Is Charles Simic afraid of death?
Yes, Charles Simic fears death.
Does he pray to the Lord above?
No, he fools around with his wife.

His conscience, does it bother him much?
It drops in for a chat now and then.
Is he ready to meet his Maker?
As much as a squirrel crossing the road.

Like an empty beer can being kicked
By some youth high as a kite
Out of one dark street into another
He stumbles and falls in the meantime.

Dice

Watch them grapple with their fate
  as they hop and roll along
casting all caution to the wind
  to beat the odds

or be retrieved by a hand
  held firmly between
its thumb and forefinger
  charmed and prayed over

to find themselves airborne
  like two giddy lovers
laughing their heads off
  as they leap naked into bed

and wake in clover afterwards
  or in a roadside ditch
battered and gray like two little toes
  sticking out of an old sneaker

itching to try their luck again
  and end up--if they must--
as cat's new toy
  gravedigger's gift to his little boy

Is That You?

On Grim Reaper's knee
Bouncing like a baby
And smiling too.
No teeth, but what a grin!
Everyone's in love with you.
They say Death
Hid his face in his hood
So he could smile too.

Such at Least Is the Story

After St. Sebastian
Had his chest
Pierced by arrows
He was nursed
Back to health
By a rich widow in Rome
With the help
Of a blind servant girl
Whose soft steps
I may have heard
Entering and leaving
My room at night
And whose name
I wish I had known
To call for help in the dark.

Taking a Breather

On the steps of a palatial funeral home
Until a couple of undertakers,
Or whoever these gents happened to be,
Asked me to move, but where to?

In the shop across the street,
The three brides in the window
Swung their pretty heads my way
As if having decided to join me.

Striped pants and black tailcoats,
Pacing back and forth like crows
Over the fresh roadkill, get lost!
I'm not budging from here today.

The Joke

Too long I've sought
What I had no name for,
Till one day
I unclenched my fist

And found a grain
Of sand in it.
Whose joke is this?
I couldn't say.

My hand grew heavy
As I held it out
Like a blind beggar
Thinking he hears steps.

After Saying Your Prayer

You who are fed up with my silence,
If you are still awake at this hour,
Listen to me as I tell you why
I'm afraid of you and keep myself
Carefully hidden in some tree
Where I sit like one of your owls
Brooding as the centuries pass.
A star falls now and then in heaven.
The sea sends another surly wave
Against the rocks, telling me
To stay where I am, even though I'm God.

Ghost Ship

Those blessed moments
    that pretend
They'll stay with us forever--
Soon gone,
    without a fare-thee-well.
What's the rush?
    I heard myself say.

You have the right
    to remain silent,
The night told me
    as I sat in bed
Hatching plans
    on how to hold the next
Captive in my head.

I recall a window thrown open
    one summer day
On a grand view of the bay
    and a cloud in all that blue
As pale as the horse
    Death likes to ride.

Always happy to shoot the breeze,
    that lone cloud
Was telling me
    as it drifted out to sea,
Toward some
    ship on the horizon,

That had already
    set sail
And was about to vanish
    out of sight,
On the way to some port
    and country
Without name.

    A ghost ship,
Most surely,
    but mine all the same.

Last Picnic

Before the fall rains arrive,
Let's have one more picnic,
Now that the leaves are turning color
And the grass is still green in places.

Bread, cheese and some black grapes
Ought to be enough,
And a bottle of wine to toast the crows
Puzzled to find us sitting here.

If it gets cold--and it will--I'll hold you close.
Night will come early.
We'll study the sky hoping for a full moon
To light our way,

And if there isn't one, we'll put all our trust
In your book of matches
And my sense of direction
As we go looking for home.

ACKNOWLEDGMENTS

These poems were published in the following literary magazines, to whose editors grateful acknowledgment is made: *The New York Review of Books, London Review of Books, The Southern Review, Conduit, Field, Literary Matters, The Harvard Advocate, The Threepenny Review,* and *Salmagundi.*